MY PERSONAL DICTIONARY

FIFTH EDITION

This book belongs to:

____

OXFORD
UNIVERSITY PRESS

Top 50 words
in alphabetical order

a
and
are
at
because
but
can
dad
day
for
fun
go
got
had
have
he
her
home
house
I
in
is
it
like
love
me
mum
my
of
on
one
play
said
saw
she
so
that
the
then
there
they
time
to
was
we
weekend
went
when
with
you

The alphabet

Aa
Bb
Cc
Dd
Ee
Ff
Gg
Hh
Ii
Jj
Kk
Ll
Mm
Nn
Oo
Pp
Qq
Rr
Ss
Tt
Uu
Vv
Ww
Xx
Yy
Zz

Aa

aeroplane

ant

apple

a	any	
about	are	
after	around	
afternoon	as	
again	asked	
ago	asleep	
all	at	
also	ate	
always	aunty	
am	away	
amazing	awesome	
an		
and		
animal		
another		

bath

bridge

bus

- baby
- back
- bad
- bag
- ball
- band
- be
- beach
- beautiful
- because
- bed
- been
- before
- best
- better
- big
- bike
- bird
- birthday
- bit
- black
- blue
- book
- bought
- box
- boy
- breakfast
- broke
- brother
- brought
- brown
- bubble
- but
- buy
- by

Aa
Bb
Cc
Dd
Ee
Ff
Gg
Hh
Ii
Jj
Kk
Ll
Mm
Nn
Oo
Pp
Qq
Rr
Ss
Tt
Uu
Vv
Ww
Xx
Yy
Zz

Cc

cat

chair

coin

cage	clothes	
cake	clown	
called	cold	
came	colour	
can	come	
can't	coming	
car	computer	
castle	cool	
cheese	could	
chicken	couldn't	
chips	cousin	
chocolate	cow	
city	crazy	
class	cry	
climb	cute	

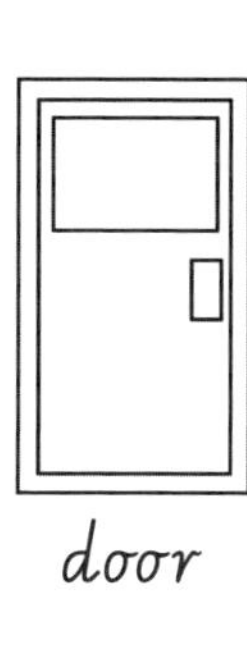

dad	don't	
dance	doom	
dark	down	
day	dragon	
dead	dress	
dear	drink	
decide	dull	
did		
didn't		
died		
different		
dinner		
dinosaur		
do		
doll		

Aa Bb Cc Dd Ee Ff Gg Hh Ii Jj Kk Ll Mm Nn Oo Pp Qq Rr Ss Tt Uu Vv Ww Xx Yy Zz

Aa Bb Cc Dd Ee Ff Gg Hh Ii Jj Kk Ll Mm Nn Oo Pp Qq Rr Ss Tt Uu Vv Ww Xx Yy Zz

Ee

eagle

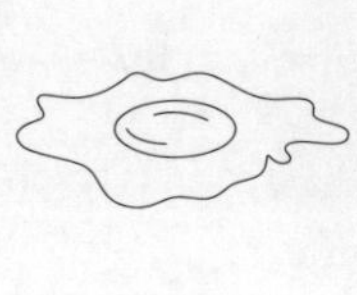
egg

elephant

each	every	
ear	everyone	
Earth	everything	
easy	evil	
eat	excited	
echidna	excursion	
edge	experiment	
eight	explore	
either	eye	
emu		
end		
enjoy		
enter		
even		
ever		

fish

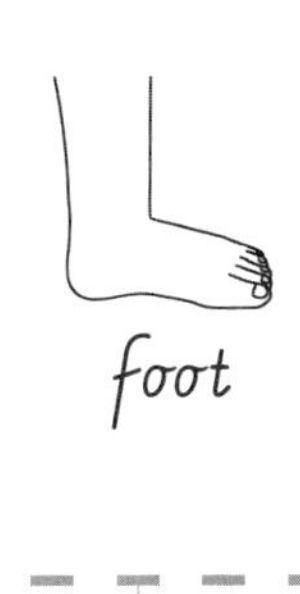

foot

frog

face	first	from
fairy	fist	fruit
family	five	fun
far	flew	funny
farm	flower	
fast	fly	
father	food	
favourite	footy	
fell	for	
felt	forest	
fight	found	
finally	four	
find	fox	
finish	Friday	
fire	friend	

Aa
Bb
Cc
Dd
Ee
Ff
Gg
Hh
Ii
Jj
Kk
Ll
Mm
Nn
Oo
Pp
Qq
Rr
Ss
Tt
Uu
Vv
Ww
Xx
Yy
Zz

Gg

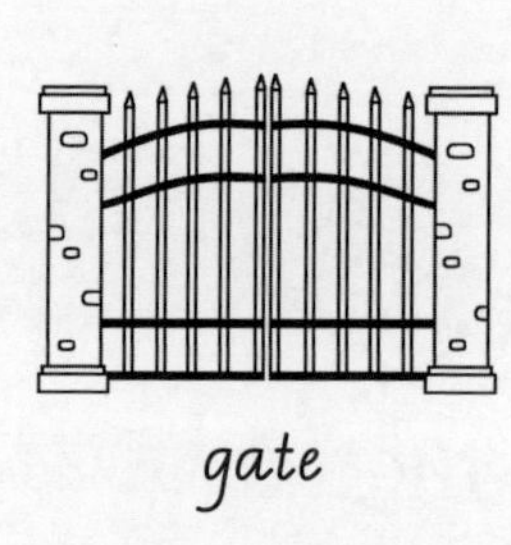

gate

giraffe

guitar

game	grandma	
garden	grandpa	
gave	grapes	
get	grass	
getting	great	
ghost	green	
giant	grow	
girl	guinea pig	
give		
go		
goes		
going		
gold		
good		
got		

horse

hose

house

had	here	hungry
hair	hi	hurt
half	hide	
hammer	high	
hand	hill	
happened	him	
happy	his	
has	hit	
have	hole	
having	holiday	
he	home	
head	honey	
hear	hope	
help	hot	
her	how	

Aa Bb Cc Dd Ee Ff Gg Hh Ii Jj Kk Ll Mm Nn Oo Pp Qq Rr Ss Tt Uu Vv Ww Xx Yy Zz

ice

ice cream

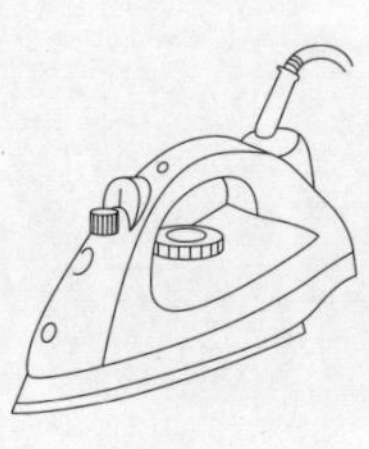
iron

iceberg	interesting	
idea	into	
if	invisible	
ignore	invite	
I'll	is	
I'm	it	
imagine	itch	
important	item	
in	it's	
include	its	
information		
ingredients		
insect		
inside		
instructions		

jelly

jug

jumper

jacket	jump	
jam	jungle	
jar	junior	
jazz	junk	
jealous	just	
jewellery		
job		
join		
joke		
journal		
journey		
joy		
judge		
juggle		
juice		

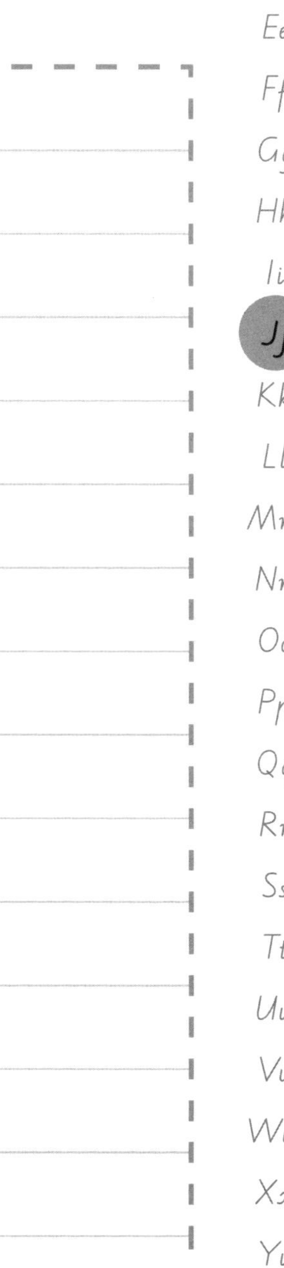

Kk

key

king

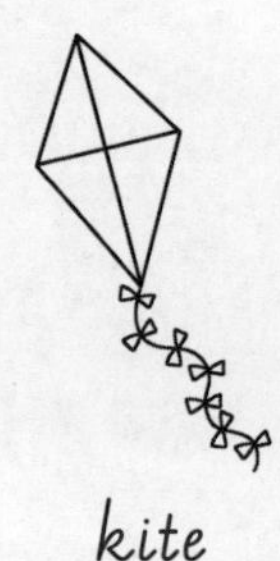
kite

kangaroo	kiss	
karate	kitchen	
keen	kitten	
keep	knee	
kennel	knife	
kept	knock	
keyring	know	
kick	koala	
kid	kookaburra	
kill		
kilometre		
kind		
kindergarten		
kindness		
king		

letter

lion

lock

ladder	light	
land	like	
language	line	
large	listen	
last	little	
late	live	
later	lolly	
laugh	long	
leaf	look	
learn	lost	
leave	lot	
left	love	
leg	lunch	
let		
life		

Aa Bb Cc Dd Ee Ff Gg Hh Ii Jj Kk Ll Mm Nn Oo Pp Qq Rr Ss Tt Uu Vv Ww Xx Yy Zz

Mm

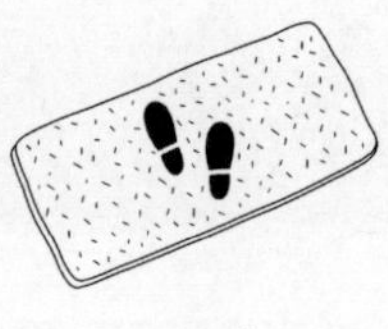
mat

mouse

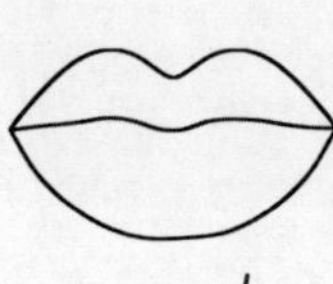
mouth

made	money	my
magic	monkey	
make	monster	
man	moon	
many	more	
map	morning	
match	most	
me	mother	
mean	motorbike	
met	movie	
middle	Mr	
might	Ms	
milk	much	
miss	mum	
Monday	music	

nail

nest

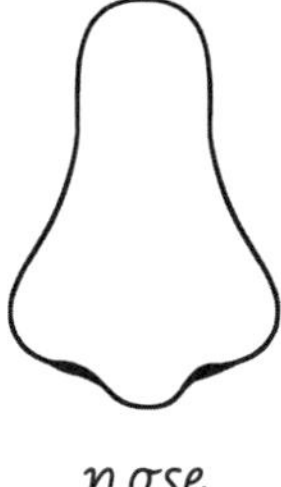
nose

name	night	
nap	nine	
narrow	no	
native	noise	
natural	normal	
necklace	north	
need	not	
nervous	nothing	
net	now	
netball	number	
never		
new		
newspaper		
next		
nice		

Aa Bb Cc Dd Ee Ff Gg Hh Ii Jj Kk Ll Mm Nn Oo Pp Qq Rr Ss Tt Uu Vv Ww Xx Yy Zz

Oo

octopus

onion

origami

object	option	
ocean	or	
o'clock	order	
of	other	
off	ouch	
office	our	
oh	out	
okay	outside	
old	oven	
on	over	
once	own	
one		
only		
open		
opposite		

pig

pin

present

pack	place	
paint	plane	
pair	play	
paper	playground	
park	police	
party	pool	
pencil	pray	
people	pretty	
person	prince	
pet	princess	
phone	puppy	
photo	put	
pick		
pink		
pizza		

Aa Bb Cc Dd Ee Ff Gg Hh Ii Jj Kk Ll Mm Nn Oo Pp Qq Rr Ss Tt Uu Vv Ww Xx Yy Zz

Qq

queen question mark quilt

quack		
quake		
quarter		
Queensland		
quest		
question		
queue		
quick		
quickly		
quiet		
quit		
quite		
quiz		
quote		

rat

robot

rocket

rabbit	right	
race	rollercoaster	
rain	room	
rainbow	routine	
ran	rug	
read	rugby	
reading	run	
ready		
really		
reason		
red		
relax		
remember		
restaurant		
ride		

Aa Bb Cc Dd Ee Ff Gg Hh Ii Jj Kk Ll Mm Nn Oo Pp Qq Rr Ss Tt Uu Vv Ww Xx Yy Zz

Aa Bb Cc Dd Ee Ff Gg Hh Ii Jj Kk Ll Mm Nn Oo Pp Qq Rr Ss Tt Uu Vv Ww Xx Yy Zz

Ss

sheep

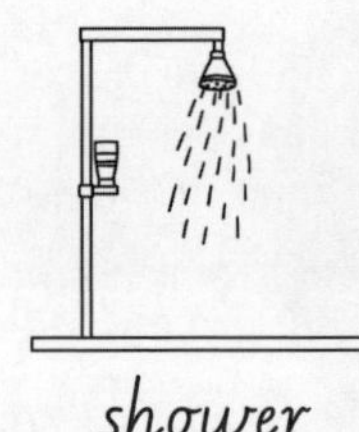
shower

snake

sad	seat	sister
safe	second	six
said	secret	sleep
same	see	sleepover
sat	set	slide
Saturday	seven	small
save	shadow	smell
saw	shark	smile
say	she	snake
scared	shop	snow
scary	should	so
school	show	soccer
score	sick	some
sea	side	someone
seal	silly	something

sock

storm

swing

sometimes		
soon		
space		
spider		
started		
stay		
still		
stop		
story		
stuff		
suddenly		
sun		
Sunday		
super		
swim		

Aa Bb Cc Dd Ee Ff Gg Hh Ii Jj Kk Ll Mm Nn Oo Pp Qq Rr Ss Tt Uu Vv Ww Xx Yy Zz

Tt

table

tablet

tap

take	their	ticket
talk	them	time
taste	then	tired
tea	there	to
teacher	they	today
team	thing	together
teeth	think	toilet
tell	thirsty	told
temperature	this	tomorrow
ten	those	too
test	thought	took
than	three	tooth
thank	threw	toothbrush
that	through	top
the	thumb	town

Aa Bb Cc Dd Ee Ff Gg Hh Ii Jj Kk Ll Mm Nn Oo Pp Qq Rr Ss Tt Uu Vv Ww Xx Yy Zz

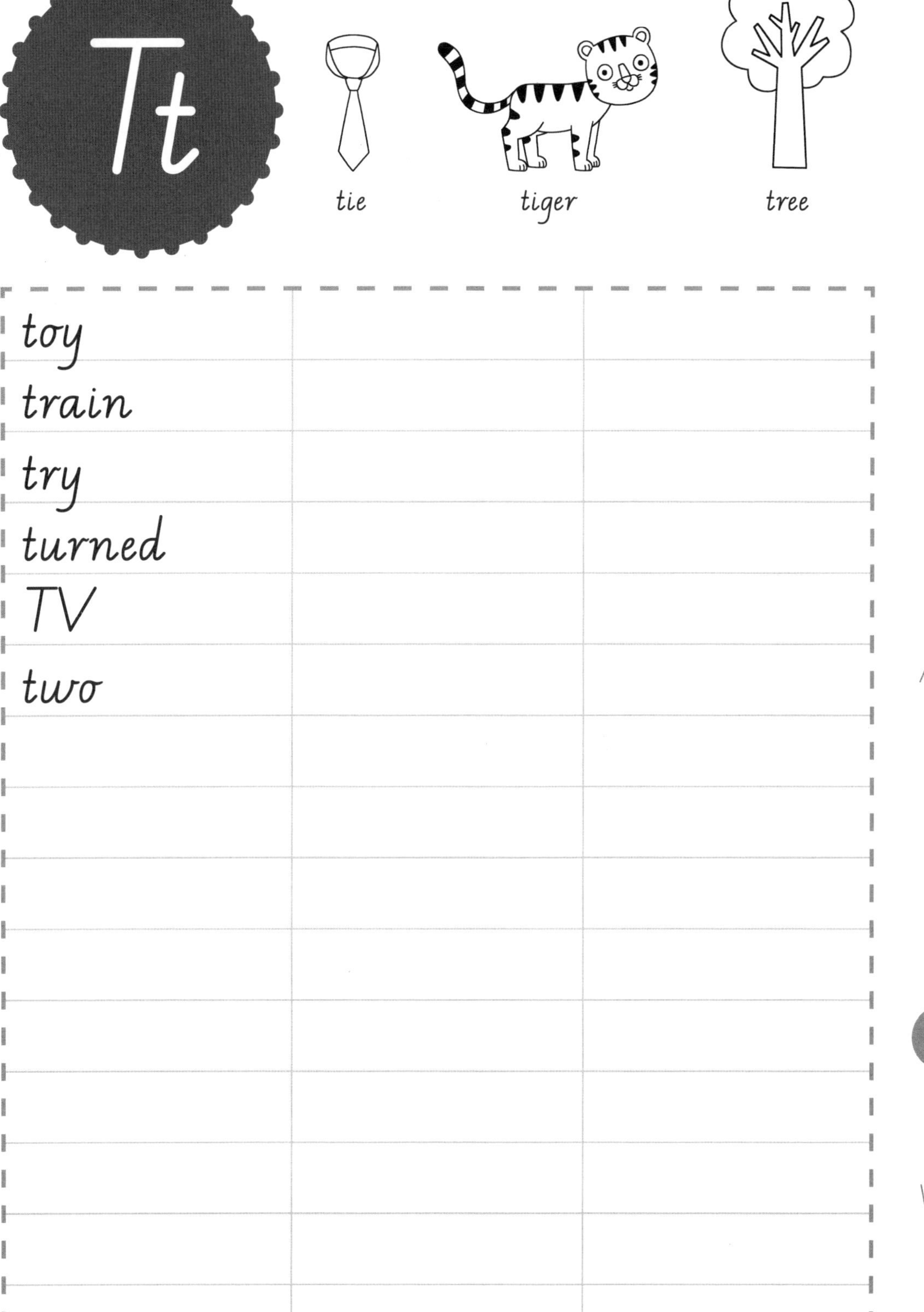

Aa Bb Cc Dd Ee Ff Gg Hh Ii Jj Kk Ll Mm Nn Oo Pp Qq Rr Ss **Tt** Uu Vv Ww Xx Yy Zz

Aa
Bb
Cc
Dd
Ee
Ff
Gg
Hh
Ii
Jj
Kk
Ll
Mm
Nn
Oo
Pp
Qq
Rr
Ss
Tt
Uu
Vv
Ww
Xx
Yy
Zz

Uu

umbrella

umpire

unicorn

ugly	use	
uncle	useful	
under	usually	
understand		
undo		
unfair		
uniform		
unit		
universe		
until		
up		
update		
upon		
upset		
us		

van

vegetables

volcano

vacuum	volunteer	
vanilla		
version		
versus		
very		
vet		
video		
view		
villain		
vine		
virus		
vision		
visit		
visitor		
volume		

Ww

whale

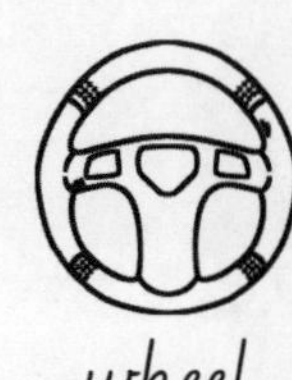
wheel

worm

wait	what	woman
walk	when	won
want	where	wood
was	which	work
wasn't	while	world
watch	white	would
water	who	write
way	whole	
we	why	
Wednesday	will	
week	win	
weekend	wish	
well	with	
went	woke	
were	wolf	

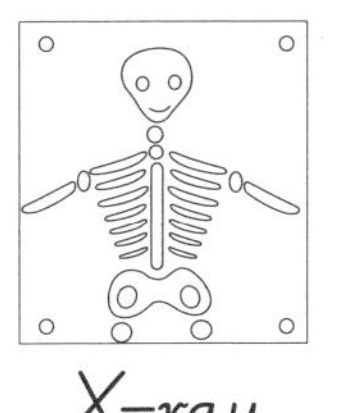

X-ray

yawn

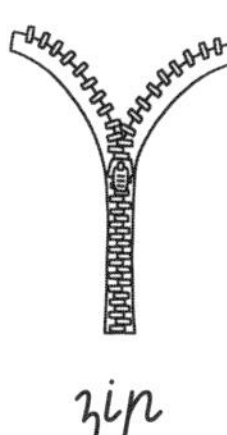

zip

xylophone	year	zebra
	yellow	zero
	yes	zoo
	yesterday	
	you	
	your	
	you're	
	yummy	

Short 'a' sound words

bat	fan	mat
can	hat	ran
cap	man	sat
clap	map	tap

Short 'e' sound words

bed	let	pet
fed	men	red
hen	net	shed
jet	pen	ten

Short 'i' sound words

bill	mill	sit
exit	pill	skip
hit	quit	spill
lip	sip	tip

Short 'o' sound words

bog	dog	log
cop	dot	mop
cot	hot	pot
crop	jog	top

Short 'u' sound words

bug	grub	rug
bun	jug	run
cub	mug	sun
fun	rub	tub

Alternative words

look

examine
glance
observe
stare
watch

said

answered
asked
replied
stated
whispered

then

afterwards
finally
next
suddenly

went

moved
ran
walked
wandered

Emotions

happy	angry
cheerful	annoyed
delighted	cross
glad	furious
joyful	mad
pleased	outraged

sad	scared
blue	afraid
down	anxious
miserable	frightened
unhappy	terrified

Homonyms

Shapes

2D shapes

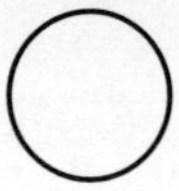

circle

crescent

diamond

heptagon

hexagon

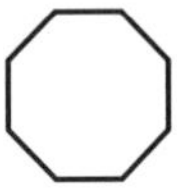

octagon

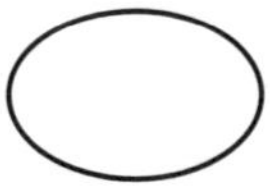

oval

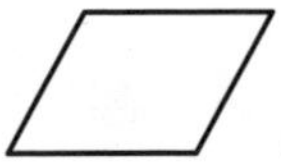

parallelogram

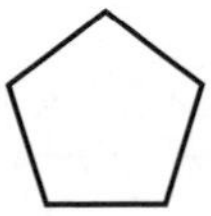

pentagon

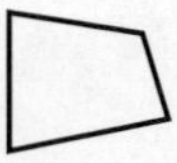

quadrilateral

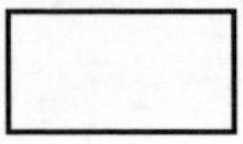

rectangle

semicircle

square

triangle

3D objects

cone

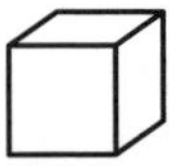

cube

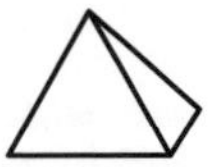

pyramid

sphere

Numbers

1 one
2 two
3 three
4 four
5 five
6 six
7 seven
8 eight
9 nine
10 ten
11 eleven
12 twelve
13 thirteen
14 fourteen
15 fifteen
16 sixteen
17 seventeen
18 eighteen
19 nineteen
20 twenty
30 thirty
40 forty
50 fifty
60 sixty
70 seventy
80 eighty
90 ninety
100 one hundred

Size

Texture

Position

I am *on top* of the box!
on top
under
beside
between
behind
in front

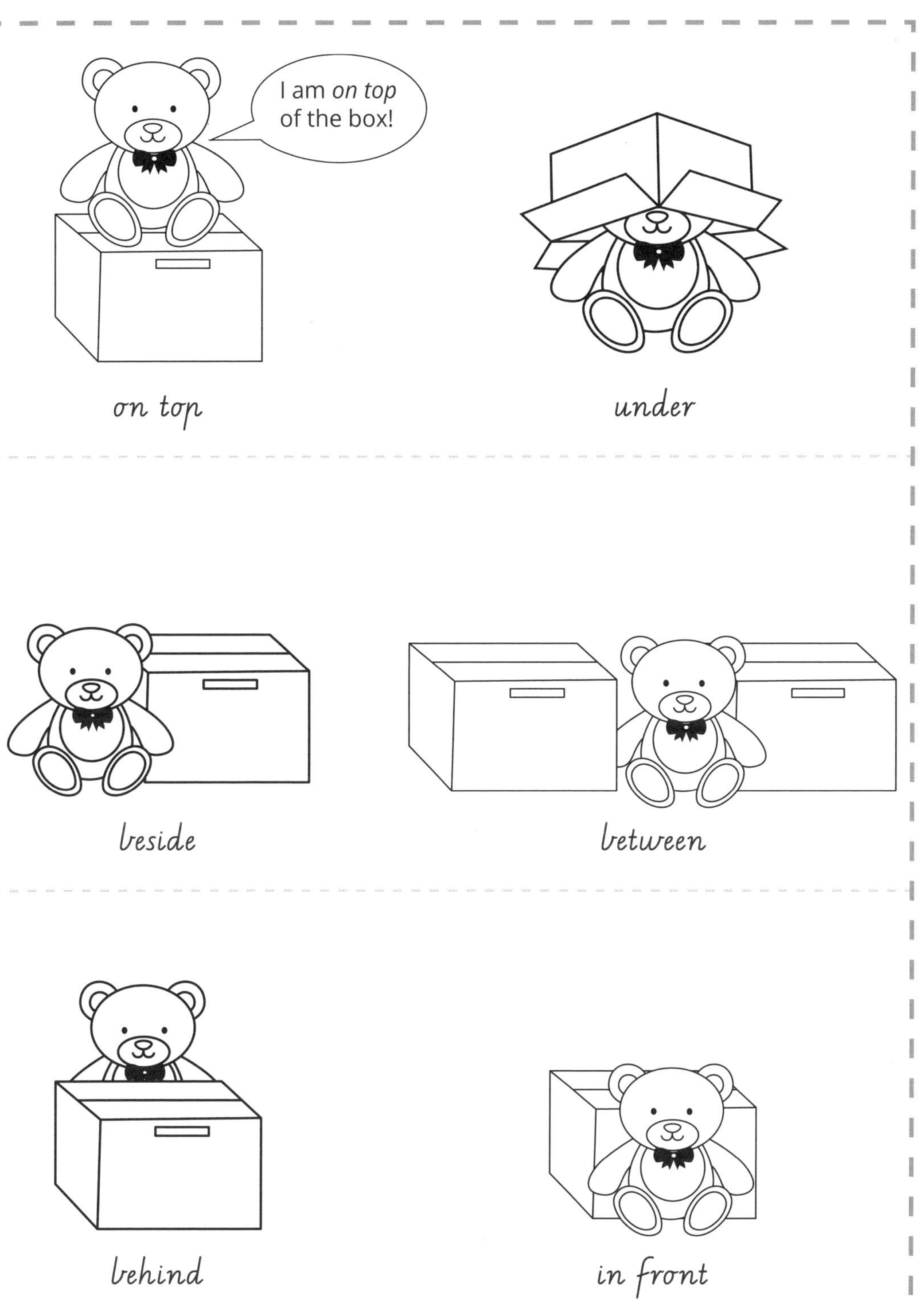

Time

second minute hour day
week fortnight month year

Days of the week

calendar

Monday
Tuesday
Wednesday
Thursday
Friday

WEEKEND

Saturday Sunday

Seasons

Summer	Autumn	Winter	Spring
December	March	June	September
January	April	July	October
February	May	August	November

Wurundjeri calendar

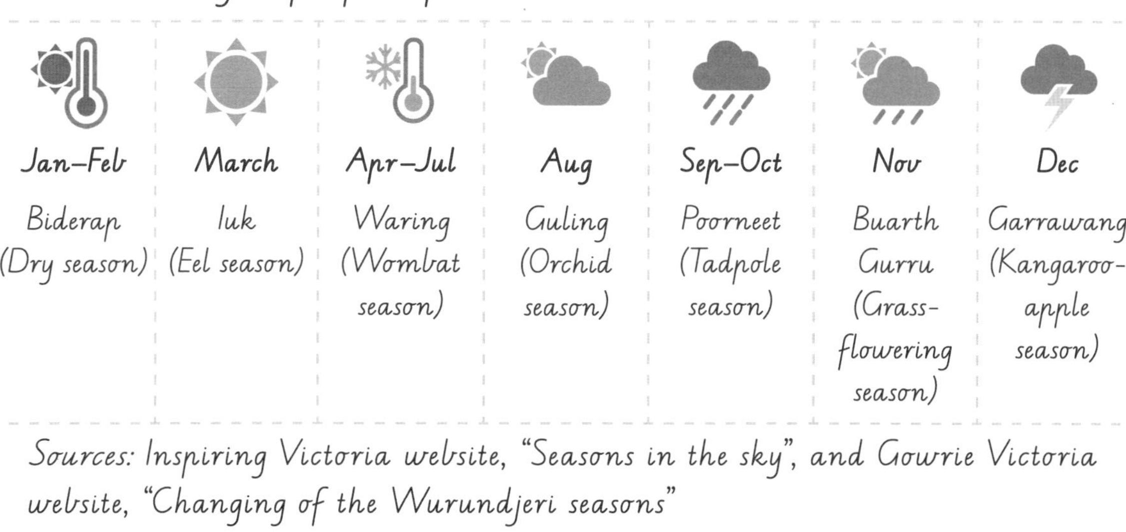

The Wurundjeri people of southern Victoria have seven seasons.

Jan–Feb	March	Apr–Jul	Aug	Sep–Oct	Nov	Dec
Biderap (Dry season)	luk (Eel season)	Waring (Wombat season)	Guling (Orchid season)	Poorneet (Tadpole season)	Buarth Gurru (Grass-flowering season)	Garrawang (Kangaroo-apple season)

Sources: Inspiring Victoria website, "Seasons in the sky", and Gowrie Victoria website, "Changing of the Wurundjeri seasons"

Classroom objects

People in our community

Australia*

crocodile
Darwin/
Garramilla
kangaroo
Western
Australia
emu
Perth/
Boorloo
cockatoo
Australian
sea lion
quokka
little
penguin

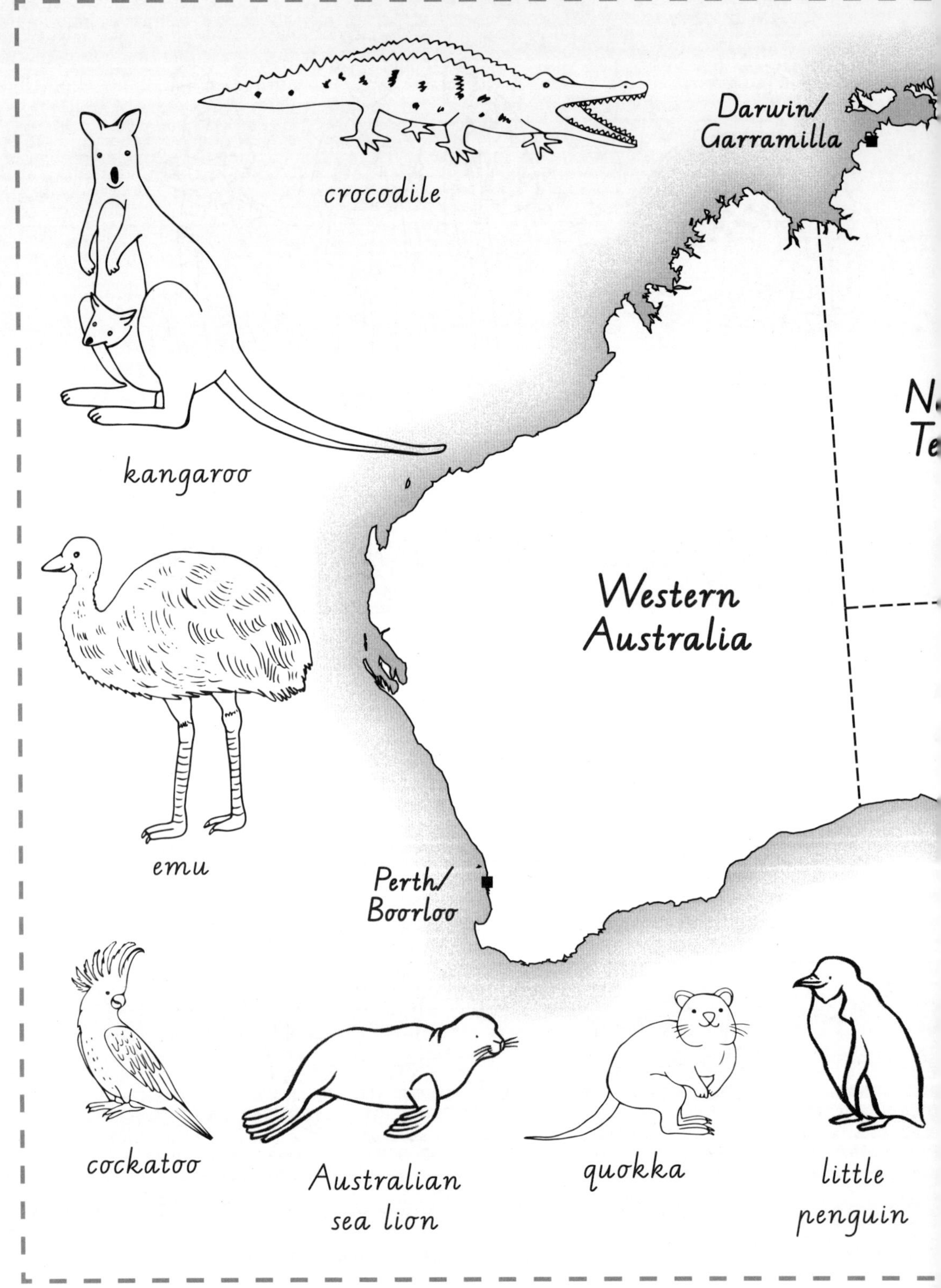

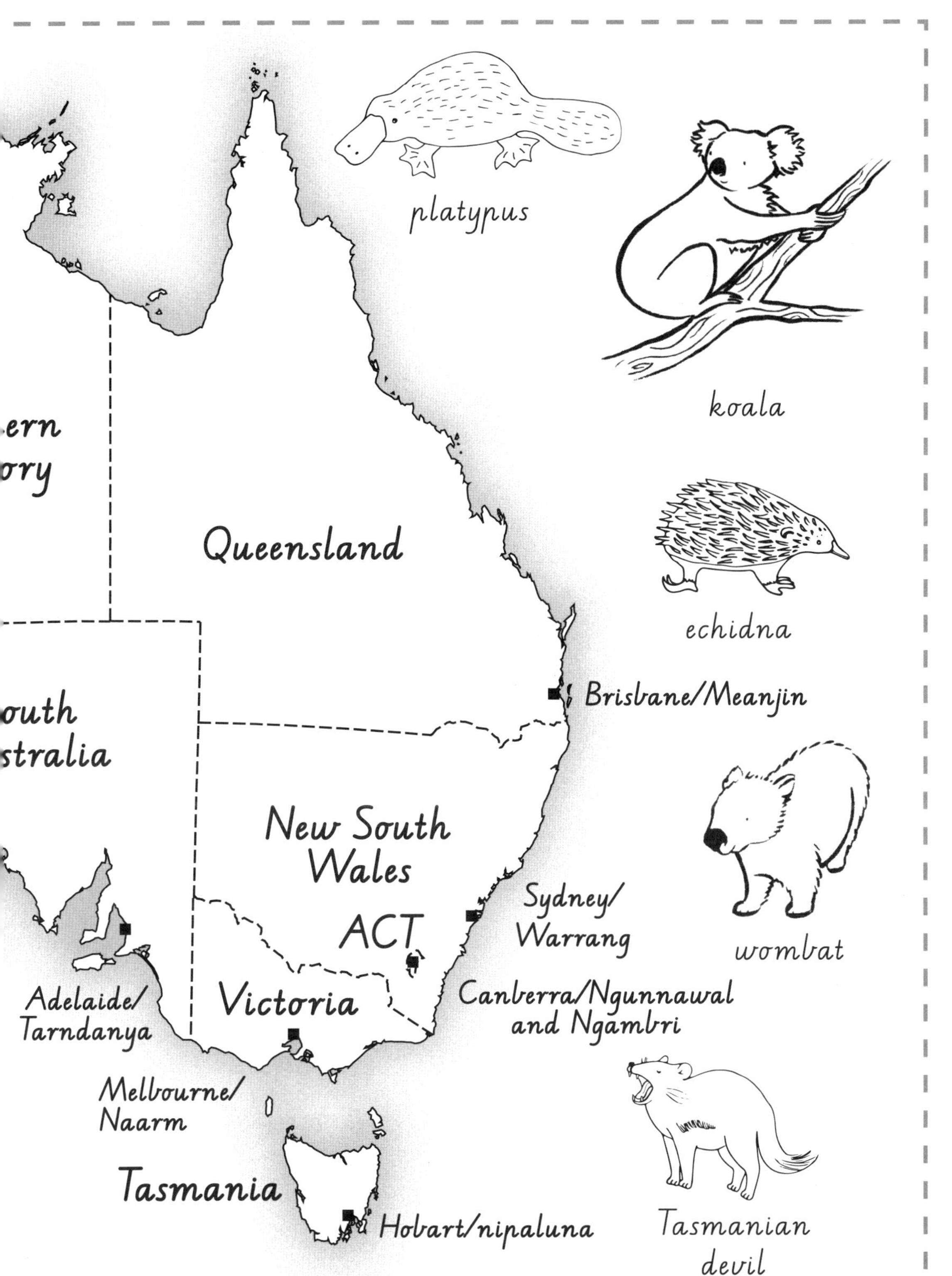

* First Nations languages are oral, and alternative spellings for these place names exist. For more information, go to the AIATSIS website or visit the Local Aboriginal Land Council.

Poem

S is for slithering snake.

P is for playful puppy.

E is for enormous eagle.

L is for large lion.

L is for little ladybird.

I is for icy ice cream.

N is for neat nest.

G is for giant giraffe.

Put the letters together – what do they spell?

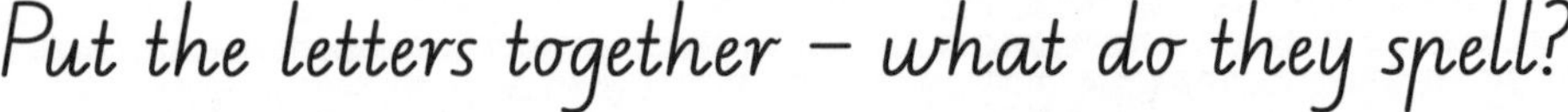